Essential Theory Of
A Course In Miracles

The Ego And Its World

Christopher R Scott

ACKNOWLEDGEMENTS

Thank you Jesus and everyone for *A Course In Miracles.*

"There are more things in Heaven and Earth… than are dreamt of in your philosophy."

William Shakespeare, Hamlet

PREFACE

A Course In Miracles was scribed by Helen Schucman via *inner dictation* from Jesus; it is a masterful blueprint of the mind—expressed in Biblical language—that uniquely shines light upon the ego and its obfuscated edifice, and its purpose is to bring one's awareness back to truth by undoing one's false perceptions, beliefs, and wishes.

Preface p. viii

About This Book

This book elucidates the Course's radical clarifications of what the ego is: its origins and its substructure, how it makes its world of fear, and its methods of deception whereby one holds its dark madness before one's true Joy; all text in italics is quotation from *A Course In Miracles*.

[Text/Workbook/Manual_chapter_section_paragraph.sentence]

TABLE OF CONTENTS

Chapter 3

INTRODUCTION

The ego and its world of division is the idea of separation—cultivated from one's desire for this—that seeks opposition to what one's Reality Is: Heaven; the ego is a *miscreation* of mind and an aberration of one's identity: *This place of darkness is not your home.*

T 3 IV 5.10   T 20 VI 7.5

1

Chapter 1

the real power of the mind

Mind reaches to itself; in truth there exists only Mind and Thought: *God's Will is Thought;* there is no physical "non-thought" that exists inherently of itself apart from the mind, and therefore, while perhaps difficult to accept, this world is an imagined mental picture of ideas, made of, in and by the mind: *The mind is very powerful, and it never loses its creative force.*

T 2 VI 9.3   T 18 VI 8.5   T 8 VI 7.3   T 2 VI 9.5

I *Heaven is... an awareness of perfect oneness*

The truth is simple; it is one, without an opposite; there must be only One Truth because multiple "truths", or differences, clearly cannot all be true: *The Holy Trinity is holy **because** It is One*; and, only the truth—oneness—exists, as what is a lie has no substance or reality.

T 18 VI 1.5-6   T 26 III 1.8   T 8 IV 8.9

II *God's Will is One*

Mind is one; God the Father creates by extending Himself, and this extension is His Son: *You are the Son of God*; the Father (Cause) can never be separate from Himself, His Son (Effect): *Cause and effect are one*; thus, what is separated from Cause is not one and is not real.

T 16 VII 6.10   T 13 VIII 4.2   W 64 3.4   T 19 IV A 3.5

III   *Everything is an idea*

As there is only Mind—*there is nothing outside it*—there must also only be ideas, yet not all ideas, such as those that depict form which is seen to be apart from the mind and thus opposing it, are real except in fantasy because only what God Creates **Is**: *God's Will... cannot be contradicted **by** thought.*

T 5 I 2.4   T 18 VI 8.8   T 8 VI 7.3

IV *mind cannot attack or be attacked*

Because cause and effect are one and inseparable, any attack that has no effect also has no cause and therefore has not really occurred: *...what has no effect does not exist*; so, since ideas, in mind, cannot be killed or harmed (effect) by other ideas, ideas and mind cannot attack (cause): *This Mind is invincible because it is undivided.*

T 7 VIII 4.3   T 11 V 2.5   T 8 V 1.8

V   Salvation comes from my one Self

Only that whole part of one's mind that is of God brings Peace and Love and Joy; the other part of the mind—the ego—that "makes" itself by splitting off from Cause harbors only pain and fear cloaked in many, many guises: *The fear is seen within, without, or both. Or it can be disguised in pleasant form.*

W 96   T 29 IV 2.3-4

Chapter 2

Your mind is capable of creating worlds

The rebellious aspect of the Son of God's mind (beyond the body, time and space) first imagines, then perceives, this world—*God did not create it*—and one is capable of this because, being part of God, one's mind is just like one's Father's: *Like Him,* you *are "always"; in His Mind and with a mind like His.*

T 10 V 9.11   M CT 4 1.2   T 9 VI 7.3

I The Ego

The ego is the deluded part of one's mind, birthed by the erroneous idea that truth can be questioned and divided, and that "something else" apart from Oneness is possible: *The ego is the questioning aspect of the post-separation self...*; and: *The ego is the part of the mind that believes in division.*

T 3 IV 3.1   T 5 V 3.1

II   The Authority Problem

The authority problem is the father of the ego; it is the valuing of the fantasy of separation over the union of Reality;   it is the wish, choice, and willingness to be one's own god; it is an alien will in opposition to God's Will: *...the authority problem is based on the concept of usurping God's power.*

T 5 V 3.3

III   *Your mind is split*

To be "living" its dream of death and division, the ego mind must believe itself split off from Life which is represented by the Holy Spirit—*the Holy Spirit is part of you*—and this is to seemingly break up the unity of Creator and Created, or of: ...*cause and effect; the most fundamental law there is.*

T 3 VII 4.11   T 16 III 5.1   T 2 VII 1.4

IV   *The ego is insane*

One must believe in the unreal to "inhabit" a world which is not Real: *...he can delude himself... and pass from mere imaging into belief and into madness, quite convinced that where he would prefer to be, he **is**.*

W II 12 2.1   T 26 V 6.10

V   *All your time is spent dreaming*

Dreaming occurs in sleep, and whomever dreams he resides in a separate body-world-psyche outside and apart from his Self **is** asleep: *When the mind elects to be what it is not... it merely seems to go to sleep awhile.*

T 18 II 5.12   W167 9.2

VI *your secret dream which you do not perceive*

A Son of God who values his authority problem 'up'loads it into a clandestine fantasy dream dreamed to make separation from his Father seem real, and this can only be implemented through ideas of attack and death, ie.: *What is not love is murder.*

T 27 VII 11.7   T 23 IV 1.10

A.   *you sought a blackness*

To become the father of oneself one must first "destroy" one's True Father and His Oneness, His Kindness, His Joy, His Mercy, His Goodness, His Eternal Gentleness, His Holiness, His Love; the recalcitrant *son of man* can only exist by "conflict" with His Peace.

T 18 III 1.5   T 24 VII 11.8

i.   Faithlessness

Faithlessness is not the lack of faith—for that is impossible—but rather it is faith in what does not exist; one misplaces one's desire, decision and willingness to make-believe that it is possible to be what one is not.

T 21 III 5.2

B.   *to attack is to separate*

The idea of attack—inconceivable in Heaven—was *carefully contrived* to "banish" Joy: *Into eternity, where all is one, there crept a tiny, mad idea, at which the Son of God remembered not to laugh.*

T 8 VII 12.1   T 16 V 15.4   T 27 VIII 6.2

C. *Attack and sin are bound as one illusion*

While ideas cannot die or be harmed, they can seemingly be disposed of, and for this the ego "joins" attack with sin; sin, another imagined concept, outcasts, or "kills", an idea via attack: *Sin is belief attack can be projected outside the mind where the belief arose.*

T 25 V 1.3   T 26 VII 12.2

D. *What else but sin could be the source of guilt...?*

Sin,—the outward attack idea to exile and destroy,—can go nowhere else but "back" to the one mind that fancies it; this perceived boomerang is guilt, an incoming attack thought of division, condemnation and loathing: *...you believed that attack could be directed outward, and returned from outside to within.*

W 259 11.4   W 196 10.3

E.   *guilt... is the belief in sin*

Now, as there is an "outside attacking me", does sin's separation seem to be proven and made believable: one's attacking "original sin" thought— since replaced and forgotten—has indeed been projected "out" of one's mind because it is seen to be outside and coming from an "other".

T 5 V 4.9

F. *ideas can leave their source*

By guilt is sin-separation actualized and made "real" such that God's Son the effect does not recognize his Cause: *Guilt remains the only thing that hides the Father*...; thus, the impossible has seemingly occurred wherein *thoughts can leave the thinker's mind*, "violating" the fundamental truth: *Ideas* [effect] *leave not their source* [cause].

W 167 4.2   T 13 IX 1.1   T 22 II 9.3   W 167 3.6

G.   *the great reversal*

Sin, the idea of separation, happened "first" in that it sired guilt—the belief in separation; yet, because guilt is what makes separation appear real, it is separation's cause, and by this does cause strangely "follow" effect: *...everything here takes a direction exactly opposite of what is true.*

T 16 V 3.6   T 18 I 6.4

H.   *effect becomes a cause; the cause, effect*

Thus by the ideas of sin and guilt does the ego seemingly manifest one's authority problem, making one the god of oneself;   God the Cause becomes the ego's "destroyed" effect, while God's Son the Effect becomes his own cause.

T 28 II 8.8

I. *to exchange Self-love for self-hate*

As the outgoing attack-to-destroy "reality" of one's sin becomes the incoming attack-to-destroy "reality" of one's guilt, another ego invention is spawned—the "reality" and dread of certain destruction, which is fear: ...*making him afraid of himself.*

T 12 III 6.3

J.   *The ego's purpose is fear*

The ego is quite literally a fearful thought; to keep one dreaming and "focused" upon separation, one's identity must be as separated—ie., guilty and afraid—and thus one's feeling fear is the agenda of the ego: *How can it preach separation without upholding it through fear...?*

T 5 V 1.3   T 5 V 3.7   T 11 V 9.3

K.   *All attack is self attack*

To actualize one's authority problem to seemingly exclude God's Peace, one must attack one's Self "out" of Heaven, and this self-attack is replicated here in the person-body-world via judgments, defenses, and making the world *what you wish*; these practices hurt you because they are all your gifts of exclusion, such that: *you give but to yourself*; thus: *If I defend myself I am attacked.*

T 10 II 5.1   T 18 II 3.7   W 187 6.1   W 135

L. *but this you are not willing to accept*

Because one constructs the ego by attack and hatred—*You made the ego without love*—so too does the ego perceive its maker by them, and thus if one identifies with the ego's separateness one must also see one's creator as hateful: *A creator* [cause] *wholly unlike his creation* [effect] *is inconceivable*; therefore, instead of knowing the Love of God, now does one falsely perceive Him with terror: *In the attack, God is assigned the attributes of the ego, while the ego appears to take on the attributes of God.*

T 18 II 4.6   T 6 IV 2.3   W 72 4.6   W 72 1.2

M. *that one error... seemed to cast you out of Heaven*

The fear of God, "His wrath", and "His quest" for your annihilation—all one's imaginary friends within one's mind—is the means whereby the ego blocks out one's only true Help, and sets one fleeing on a fruitless pursuit for safety and salvation into fantasy "outside"; and, for these external escapades the ego dreams a second dream...

T 18 I 5.6

VII *The dreaming of the world... the part you see*

To "heal" the mind's separation anxiety, felt as incoming attack and impending doom by God's "cold cruel hand", the ego conjures an "outside-of-the-mind" experience: *...a place where God could enter not, and where His Son could separate from Him.*

T 27 VII 11.6-7 W II 3 2.4

A. *the guilt is so acute that it must be projected*

The self-attack and fear one makes to sever from Oneness is so intolerable to the mind that orchestrates them that the mind then hallucinates—literally—an "outside" where it can seemingly deposit and dispose of its pain; this process of the transference of one's unwanted conflicts to an "other" outside is called projection.

T 5 V 3.11

B.   *The dream of guilt*

Just as the ego uses self-attack to "cast away" God, so too must it also use self-attack to project out its resultant guilt; for this reason one must view one's projected world of separation as a guilty testimony to inner assault, death and fear: *...because your attack thoughts will be projected, you will fear attack.*

T 27 VII 14.6   W 26 2.1

C. *The world was made as an attack on God*

The cause of the world is: one's authority problem; one's desire for death, or that which is apart from Life; one's obsession to fragment the natural Oneness of mind onto a world of infinitudes, and by this is one's defense of a special world really one's defense of the attack; the dream of murder, and its world, must therefore be: *...your protest against reality, and your fixed and insane idea that you can change it.*

W II 3 2.1   T 18 II 5.15

D. *The world arose to hide it*

The person-body-world is an "outside-the-mind" respite where one, who values the ego over God, can imagine safety from God's "eternal damnation" which seems to unrelentingly foment torment within: *And he must stand alone in his protection, and make himself a shield to keep him safe from fury that can never be abated, and vengeance that can never be satisfied.*

T 18 I 6.2 M 17 5.9

E. *Fear has made everything you think you see*

As the motive and cause of the body-world is fear, so too must be its effect: *For every dream is but a dream of fear, no matter what the form it seems to take;* yet, as *fear is both a fragmented and a fragmenting emotion,* the body-psyche-world is perceived as splintered multiplicity "outside" and apart from the one ego mind which secretly imagines it.

W 130 4.1   T 29 IV 2.2   T 18 I 3.3

F.   *The body is a limit*

The body is a vehicle for "proof" of separation from one's Creator; instead of being an eternal, unlimited idea of Peace and having everything always, now is one confined to a tiny segment of time, space, and "life" whereby one's mind is caused by, separated in, and witnessed to *a wall of flesh.*

T 18 VI 8.2   T 20 VI 11.2

G. *bodies... a concrete form of fear*

Fear constricts, constrains, confines and condemns, and this is why one's home "outside" of the mind appears as finite and final, vulnerable and victimized; the body, like all unreal fabrications of the mind, is a fearful effect: *The body... is the result of a tiny, mad idea of corruption...*; it is also, as are all illusions, a deception: *Can you who see yourself within a body know yourself as an idea?*

W 161 5.2   T 19 IV C i 5.2,6   T 18 VIII 1.5

H.   *the scapegoat for guilt*

Instead of seeing what and where its error lies, the ego-mind deflects its self-attack upon the body: *You have displaced your guilt to your body from your mind*; therefore guilt is the cause of sickness and decline: *Its* [mind's] *guilt, which keeps it separate, is projected to the body, which suffers and dies because it is attacked to hold the separation in the mind...*

T 18 VI 6.1, 2.5, 3.4

I.   *the body is to attack with*

Because mind and ideas cannot attack or be attacked, the sickened mind must act out its fantasies of war by ingeniously inventing ideas that can morph into "non-ideas" which "leave" the mind by cloaking into form and bodies—*The body is outside you* [mind];   now, disguised in rotting frailty, are the thoughts of death and battle clearly demonstrable and thus made "victor" over the Thought of Peace: *Mind cannot attack, but it can make fantasies and direct the body to act them out.*

T 8 VIII 1.5   T 18 VI 9.1, 3.5

J.   *Made to be fearful*

To prove its omnipotence over Joy, the ego envisions a surrogate: *...a frightened mouse that would attack the universe*; this is its fleeting *little speck of dust* that demonstrates "life apart from God": *Yet is it joy to look upon decay and madness, and believe this crumbling thing, with flesh already loosened from the bone and sightless holes for eyes, is like yourself?*

W II 5 3.4   T 22 V 4.3   T 18 VIII 3.2   T 24 V 4.8

K.   *There is no world!*

The world is real only as hallucinations are: *the great projection* does not exist because it is a dreamed of imaged shadow of oneself that is sustained only by the wish of the dreamer; *There is no world because it is a thought apart from God, and made to separate the Father and the Son...*; and, the world cannot be real because, again (section 1 IV), it is the progeny of the futile and senseless aspiration to make "ideas die": *The world is an illusion.*

W 132 6.2   T 22 II 10.1 W 132 13.1   W 155 2.1

L. *"external reality" is a pictorial representation of your own attack thoughts*

Whatever is perceived is separate—being "from" the outside—and so must it originate from one's idea of attack-to-separate before it is returned and seen thus as incoming attack; therefore, all that one perceives as being outside of one's mind is none other than one's own sin-guilt-fear: *Who sees a brother as a body sees him as fear's symbol. And he will attack...*

W 23 3.1-2   W 161 8.1.2

M.   *backwards and upside down*

Since separation causes cause and effect to be reversed in the mind (section 2 VI G), so does the mind's seen dream follow this; now, the outside body-brain-world is the cause of the mind's thoughts instead of the mind causing them, which is as it is.

T 18 I 6.4

N.   *The body is the ego's idol*

In idolatry one first displaces "out" the power of one's mind onto the body-world;   then, in "worship", one attempts to reclaim and introject this outside power wherein one can thus be magically sustained and be kept "alive" apart from Life.

T 20 VI 11.1

O. *I see only the past*

Time is another concocted idea the ego uses to escape the reality of eternity; the world's dreams are made of the ancient past cast long ago, which is replayed over and over in seeming endless variations to keep oneself dreaming of the guilty nonexistent: *For if what has been* [past guilt] *will be punished, the ego's continuity is guaranteed.*

W 7   T 13 I 8.7

P. *sacrifice... the price that must be paid*

Loss by sacrifice is both a keystone and a cornerstone of the ego; it is the idea that immolation makes existence whereby "I live by your death" and "I must give up to gain"; it births innocence—life—from victimhood, which is the necessary ego device to direct guilt outward: "you are the cause my deprivation and pain, thus are your hands bloodied and mine pure"; sacrifice hails from the original "slaughtering" of Paradise to sate the serpent of separation; and, like all of the ego, it is entirely fiction, as Oneness cannot lose anything, ever: *Sacrifice is a notion totally unknown to God.*

M 13 5.1-2   T 3 I 4.1

VIII *foolish guardians of mad illusions*

Because the ego's version of reality is exclusively false and deranged, it must construct formidable bulwarks of more fantasy to defend against the dreamer from waking up to its nightmare.

W 4 VI 1.6

A. *substitution is the strongest defense the ego has*

The world begins by one's valuing, and substituting, the god of oneself over God; thus, essentially, it and its thoughts one thinks and its reality one believes in is an imposter for the Truth—a lie: *The ego's fundamental truth is to replace God.*

T 18 I 1.6   W 72 2.1

B. *making peace of chaos, joy of pain, and Heaven out of hell*

The ego's *Laws of Chaos* attempt to overturn God's Laws of Mind by contorting them—unsuccessfully—into mangled bits of hatred, yet by the ego's "laws" does its world of wishes seemingly coalesce to power and operate one's mindless miscreant merry-go-round of phantoms and folly.

T 23 II   W 200 2.1

i.   Specialness-Hierarchy

Instead of ideas being as one and unassailable in one indivisible mind, the ego questions this and entertains the dream that ideas can inhabit different orders of truth, or value or specialness, ie., that differences apart from oneness can exist: ...*all conflict arises from the concept of levels. Only the Levels of the Trinity are capable of Unity [because They are of one Mind and one Will]*.

T 3 IV 1.6-7 II 5.5

ii. Sin-Attack

As the ego continues to run with and develop its concept of contrived differences to make "my truths more true than yours", it makes-believe that ideas can attack and exclude themselves apart from each other and from their cause: *The separation is the notion of rejection.*

T 6 I 18.4

iii. Guilt-Fear

To enforce and make real its lust for separation, and because *the sender and receiver are the same*, the ego need only allow one's differential attack thoughts to follow their sole destiny of returning to, and leaving not, their source;   this, one's own incoming attack, then, is self-condemnation, or guilt, accompanied by fear, and because these conjurings are seen as outside it is they—ascribed to God by the ego—which take blame for one's frightful aloneness.

T 19 IV B *i* 14.8

iv.   Sacrifice-Jealousy

Now, verified by an indomitable "outside" antagonist, the ego continues in its drama to isolate itself by playing the role of victim, separated by forces against its will: *I am the thing you made of me, and as you look on me, you stand condemned because of what I am*; thus can the ego seemingly claim separation yet escape its consequence of guilt: *While you attack I must be innocent...*

T 31 V 5.3   T 27 VII 3.3

v.   Greed-Idolatry

Although "innocent", the ego must still avenge for what has been "stolen" and thus its grievances-to-take-back are justified; this "outside-to-be-consumed"—one's own specter, really—then is seen as salvation such that it is idolized and becomes one's *substitute for love*, yet by one's authority problem love must remain apart and not be allowed to join; it is to be perpetually chased and forever forgotten.

T 23 II 12.4

vi.   *For the ego* **is** *chaos*

…what I value is specialness over Holiness so I attack to expel my completion whose exile is made real as the attack returns to me and takes away my happiness so I must seek vengeance to reclaim it yet what I value is specialness over Holiness so I attack to expel my completion whose exile is made real as the attack returns to me and takes away my happiness so I must seek vengeance to reclaim it yet…

T 14 X 5.6

C.   The Special Relationship

For our separate specialness we project both our love and our hate—the "triumph" over Oneness and its resultant guilt—onto the "outside" with which we then either "fall in love" or inject blame, preferring, again and again, these repetitive rituals of *self-aggrandisement* and self-loathing over our truth with God: *The special love relationship is the ego's most boasted gift*; the special relationship, however, exemplifies the profundity of ego confusion if its modi are only looked upon, as it attempts the impossible: to   join   and   unite—love—via expressions of division and separation, and to banish one's guilt from one's mind by attack and condemnation.

T 17 IV 8.3   T 16 V 3.1

i. *the fantasy of destruction of love's meaning*

Love's meaning is the unbroken extension of union to all always, so, to love specific persons, things, or ideals etc. is to first separate them—and oneself— out of the mind's natural wholeness, and by this is excluded God's Love and everything else; such is the *self-betrayal* that founds perhaps the greatest ego deception of all—the gleaning of temporary happiness from the isolation and sacrifice of another: *...any seeming happiness that does not last is really fear. ... for the eternal cannot change.*

T 16 V 15.1   T 29 IX 9.2   T 22 II 3.5-6

D.   *The attraction of guilt*

Because whatever perceived as separate and outside of mind can be none other than one's own guilt, all "outside" that one is enamored with thus represents one's own attraction to this guilt: "I want my guilt that I sever myself from my Creator, and I want to see your guilt that I may yet proclaim my innocence"; and, if one desires guilt then punishment and fear are also wished for; these wishes, of course, are mostly unconscious, nevertheless they defend and strengthen one's ego whose choice for specialness **is** conscious: *The continuing decision to remain separated is the only possible reason for continuing guilt feelings*; and: *This willingness means that you do not want to be healed.*

T 19 IV A i 10.1   T 5 V 8.1   T 5 VII 3.6

E.   *Sin as an Adjustment*

The ego teaches attack and manipulation of what is outside to perfect one's sanctuary of sacrifice, yet this *idle seeking* for what is without—gaining another body, ruining a rival, having advantage, upgrading a spouse, winning this disagreement, saving the day or increasing me or my dog's memory skills—is more ego deception that can only embolden the circle of separative self-attack: *If you seek to separate out certain aspects of the totality and look to them to meet your imagined needs, you are attempting to use separation to save you. How, then, could guilt not enter?*

T 20 III   W 86 1.6   T 15 V 2.3-4

F.   *fantasy solutions*

Magic is the contrived "outside" solutions to the contrived "inside" problem,—the fear of God,—and is designed to perpetually imprison the mind with said mindless apparitions which defend against the one solution—that of seeing that oneself is the contriver of these apparitions: *The secret of salvation is but this: that you are doing this unto yourself;* and: *The body is released* [healed] *because the mind acknowledges "this is not done to me, but I am doing this."*

T 17 VI 7.6   T 27 VIII 10.1   T 28 II 12.5

G.   *Sickness... another form of guilt*

Sickness is a type of self-attack yet it *can be nothing but a dream*; it, calamity, pain, and problems of all kinds—as well as bodily-worldly pleasures, cures, triumphs and solutions—are special magical schemas designed to feed body-world identification to the mind that wants separation, thus enlivening the ego and its required fear; all of these the effects of their one cause which is the wish to dispel and barricade against God's Love: *Your purpose was to ensure that healing did not occur.*

W 140 4.2,3   W 70 4.2

H.   *vision is obscured*

As the ego's purpose is to keep one afraid, it must work ceaselessly to block one's sight to the fact that it, and all of its works, **is** fear: *Your recognition that whatever seems to separate you from God is only fear... is therefore the basic ego threat.*

T 2 V 8.4   T 11 V 10.1

I. *idols must keep hidden what you are*

Seeking for salvation through the outside is the ego's fixed alpha and omega, and it **keeps salvation outside** because the ego, quite simply, does not want one to ever have it or to know where it is: *It is in me because its Source is there. ...It is not found outside and then brought in;* and, by seeking, attacking and taking the "life" of idols from without—merely frightened effects imagined by a mind that believes in lack—does one veil who One Is within, and this ego defense begins with judgment: *I make all things my enemies, so that my anger is justified and my attacks* [plunders] *are warranted... I have done this to defend a thought system that has hurt me.*

T 30 II 11.8   W 86 1.6   W 85 3.3,6   W 51 5.3,5

J. *what you really want to hide*

The whole of the worldly fantasy rests on the ungodly fantasy that God hates us for what we do or have done, and thus we must hide here from His "vengeance" by blaming others; yet to defend "my" world is to defend this delusion which is to defend against His Grace, for it is His Love that we as egos are most terrified of: *Your fear of attack is nothing compared to your fear of love. ...your savage wish to kill God's Son... caused the separation, and you have protected it because you do not want the separation healed.*

T 13 III 2.9,3-5

IX   *God knows not form*

For sight of form means understanding has been obscured; all things seen or thought to be outside— death, illnesses, situations, "parallel" universes, pasts-futures, *the bodies of those who are not there*, etc.—do not exist autonomously of themselves but rather, like everything, they are ideas in and of the mind; these are the ego's "anti-ideas" because they seem to reside apart from—and be not caused by— the mind which thinks and perceives them, and they are not of God: *God does not contradict* [separate] *Himself...*

T 30 III 4.5   T 22 III 6.8   T 17 III 3.1   T 8 VI 7.5

X   *You choose your dreams*

The ego world and its *miserable parody of life* does not happen to us: *You are the dreamer of the world of dreams*; it is by our fallen faith that we believe in the false, and illusions become our vision of truth: ...*what you see in dreams you think is real while you are asleep.*

T 27 VII 13.1   W 121 4.2   T 18 II 5.12   T 10 I 2.1.5

XI   *this carefully prepared arena, where angry animals seek for prey*

The ego was engineered to elude Peace; by this is its existence defined by perpetual battles and perennial strife within the boundary of hopes randomly gained and lost, all which are frantic attempts to delay and parry—yet kiss—the unavoidable terminus presented by the person-body-world; yet *This Need Not Be* if it is not one's wish: *While you want it* [world] *you will see it; when you no longer want it, it will not be there for you to see.*

W 72 4.1...T IV 4 W 32 1.5

Chapter 3

So He thought, "My Children sleep and must be awakened"

The miracle of *A Course In Miracles* is corrected vision, or healed perception, wherein one sees all—both truth and illusions—as in and of one's mind, but where truth is only wholeness and unity with one's Creator: *When you have learned that you belong to truth, it will flow lightly over you without a difference of any kind*; here miracles show that **all** of one's problems are solved not at their effects—the world—but only in the mind at their singular cause: the rejection of Authority; thus, the miracle of vision is the Holy Spirit's gentle alarm clock for this world, sounded by: *The miracle is possible when cause and consequence are brought together, not kept separate.*

T 6 V 1.8   T 13 XI 6.6   T 26 VII 14.1

I Forgiveness

By corrected belief and by corrected vision and by corrected faith—all in truth and not in illusions—is one's mind healed by the Holy Spirit; yet: *Forgiveness must be practiced...*

W 134 13.1

A.   *the end of sacrifice*

Atonement is: ***I am as God created me.*** *…This is the word of God that sets you free*; it comes not by the archaic ego religion of salvation by murder, vicarious or otherwise; God's Grace is relationship with His Only Son as You Are.

W 37 1.5   W 110 11.4,6

II The Holy Relationship

The holy relationship—*A situation is a relationship, being the joining of thoughts*—is the classroom of the miracle, and this where one practices forgiveness; the holy relationship is one's relationship with one's holiness—one's Self— extended to all and everyone by this Self, the Holy Spirit: *Once your mind is healed it radiates health, and thereby teaches healing.*

T 17 VII 3.1   T 6 V C 9.7

A.   *A common purpose*

A holy relationship is not realized by its "attainment"; rather, it is found within any special relationship where the acceptance of Peace and the abandonment of rejection—in mind—is practiced and becomes the goal; it is: *...any two who join together for learning purposes. The relationship is holy because of that purpose...*; it is where *each one learns that giving and receiving are the same,* and where the relationship is given to the Holy Spirit for His Use: *Let miracles replace all grievances.*

T 30 VII 4.1   M 2 5.3-5   W 78

III   The Holy Spirit

The Holy Spirit is that part of one's mind that can never separate from Truth; the Holy Spirit is one's Healer, Mediator and Guide who returns one back to sanity, as only by aligning oneself with the truth, and not illusions, can the truth be followed and accepted: *God is the Love in which I forgive*; and: *Nothing can prevail against a Son of God who commends his spirit into the Hands of his Father.*

W 46   T 3 II 5.1

A. *the Kingdom of God is within you*

The ego guides one to seek salvation outside via vanishing forms and certain death where its motto of *seek but do not find* is perhaps its only resonant to fact, therefore: *Seek Not Outside Yourself;* allow the mind to return to its Self and to Joy in the universe of ideas that cannot harm and that abide only in Peace and Love and Freedom of One Eternal Being which are found only where they Are,

...and God Himself will raise you from darkness into light.

W 77 3.3   W 71 4.2   T 29 VII   W 69 7.2

CONCLUSION

The ego seems real only as one attacks oneself "outside" of Reality, thus "ego-existence" here is the great omnipresent oxymoron and the king of koans, but it and its world all **seem** to exist because: *Those who choose to come to it are seeking for a place where they can be illusions, and avoid their own reality;* yet: *This world is full of miracles. ...They are the dream's alternative, the choice to be the dreamer, rather than deny the active role in making up the dream.*

W 155 2.2   T28 II 12.1,3

EPILOGUE

Truth is never outside, for the outside is outside of Life…

For truth extends inward…

There is nothing outside you.

T 18 I 6.3   T 18 VI 1.1

www.ingramcontent.com/pod-product-compliance
Lightning Source LLC
Chambersburg PA
CBHW062042280526
45788CB00003B/1076